WELL WATER:
An Experiment in Poetry

Ashley Clayton Kay

Carlin Charles Thompson

MARCKS Publishing

Copyright © 2017 by Ashley Clayton Kay

All rights reserved. No part of this publication may be reproduced, distributed, or transmitted in any form or by any means, including photocopying, recording, or other electronic or mechanical methods, without the prior written permission of the publisher, except in the case of brief quotations embodied in critical reviews and certain other noncommercial uses permitted by copyright law. For permission requests, write to the publisher, addressed "Attention: Permissions Coordinator," at the address below.

MARCKS Publishing
P.O. Box 19286
Louisville, KY 40259

www.marckspublishing.com

Printed in the United States of America
ISBN-13: 978-1-948151-01-6

First Edition

14 13 12 11 10 / 10 9 8 7 6 5 4 3 2 1

WELL WATER: AN EXPERIMENT IN POETRY

DEDICATED TO

My Dad

TABLE OF CONTENTS

PART ONE

Explaining Myself	1
Definition	4
My 10 Cents	5
Morning Music	6
Café	7
Thriving	8
Characters	9
Screened	10
Heavy Accent	11
Unrequited Bus	12
Femininity	13
Point of No Return	14
Grief	15
How I Tell It	16
Masculinity	17
Tectonics	18

PART TWO

Time Turns	23
Glance of Wine	24
Sentinel	25
Glaciers	26
Advice From Dad	27
Ice Scream	28
Inkeeping the Elderly	30
Can-Tankerous	31
Writermouse	32
Path	33
Laundry	34
Adult Birthdays	35
People of the South Wind	37
Love From Mother	38
Degrees	39

PART THREE

Confusion	43
Shower Thoughts	44
Stimuli	45
Gravity	46
Little Armored Me	47
A Year in Kansas	49
Circles	55
Seasons	57
(Ocean)	58
Third Fruit From the Window	59
A Woman, Dying	60
Denoument	61
Stairs to Nowhere	62
ABOUT THE AUTHORS	65

PART ONE

YOUTH

EXPLAINING MYSELF
A.C.K.

Instead of speaking I
Explained
Myself to people, pleasing
To gain a smile.
I went home to my mirrors and
Checked my mailbox all winter long.
I looked and looked
For my answer,
Then wrote something sad on a postcard
In cursive
Kept in a bowl of birthday cards.

Instead of speaking I
Jotted
And listened, noting
People and time, especially
The importance of Sunday afternoon.
I laughed and laughed –
Making light –
Comforting with jokes,
Performing a play of my feelings.

Instead of speaking I
Walked
Quickly and kept my secrets,
Staring at a stretch of grassy summer sideyard.
I watched and watched
Through windows
The moving clouds and crowds—
And no one traveled my way.

Instead of speaking I
Tip-toed

In the dull light
Of my friendly screen, a space
For all the forgotten Tuesdays.
I thought and thought
While driving—singing—
Later journaling unworthy
Daily hopes
For a woman,
This character of fiction.

Instead of speaking I
Stashed
Odd phrases and ideas
On floating papers, cursed when
Dug out of purses
One evening in a waning April.
I waited, bracing for their reaction:
Doubtful, always
And never hard to read—
Yet I was compelled to know how
They spelled it.

Instead of speaking I
Typed
Forever fearing the reception
Of my words
On a quiet November night.
I worked and worked
Doing jobs
With unending downtime
Where all I did was
story life.

Instead of speaking I
Assumed
I had no need to create a voice
Despite a paper trail of practiced dialogue

Inking up the ripped-out July
Of my refrigerator flip calendar.
I saw this truth so suddenly I
Shouted
Into a pillow and pondered
A poem.

DEFINITION
A.C.K.

poems are the stories
of moments

MY 10 CENTS
C.C.T.

When writing a poem –
A rhyme for a dime –
Words forever,
Thoughts of time.

MORNING MUSIC
C.C.T.

Beaming through a window,
the sun will vainly play a song,
shining over sleeping faces
as if nothing could go wrong

CAFÉ
A.C.K.

Cloud croissants –
Shapes of air:
A mushroom, a crab,
A fat derrière.

THRIVING
A.C.K.

Hallelujah, praise the sun!
Sing ruby begonias, covered in dew:
waving, bobbing in the wayward wind –
a gospel choir blown from its pew.

CHARACTERS
A.C.K.

I live the others' lives—
the ones inside my head.
Their lives are like the ones I wish
that I could live instead.

They talk to me a lot
inside my busy head.
They talk so much I have to stop
to catch just what they've said.

I hope they're always there,
rambling in my head.
Some nights I lie awake to hear them
Run lines with me in bed.

Some days I sit around
stuck inside my head.
Those days I just can't bring myself
to live my life instead.

SCREENED
A.C.K.

Hanging baskets on abandoned porch land –
like severed heads, green with spider-leg hair –
each swinging by one wired, hooky hand,
looking for me from in between
the coiffure of a cobweb fan.

HEAVY ACCENT
A.C.K.

Rubber boots on wet, loose gravel
spoken with an old English slur –
noise like a mouthful of sour sixpence –
grappling through driving rain,
dripping off a cur.

UNREQUITED BUS
A.C.K.

The bus speaks to me in loving buzzes;
it clings to me as sticky fuzzes.
I'm desperate for it at my stop
then leave it cold without a thought—
the bus loves me,
I love it not!

FEMININITY
A.C.K.

Unbroken, open eggs
like sewn buttons
made to hold
the sides and shapes of all places
at the center.

POINT OF NO RETURN
C.C.T.

Woman's womb
...like a tomb:
Creates life
...creates doom.

GRIEF
A.C.K.

How can I hug my grief
if it gives itself away
to others in their lifelong corners, darker
than my humdrum day?

HOW I TELL IT
A.C.K.

A rugged chap with a weakness for drinking
and constantly writing down all he is thinking
so into depression he kept sinking and sinking....
With one last ordeal,
I turned on my heel
(at least that's how I tell it to make it less real).

MASCULINITY
A.C.K.

Shelters formed with
rocky, rusted
metal materials
battled over
coffee.

TECTONICS
C.C.T.

Rush of wind—
      flood of Fire
Bodies in lust—
      earthen Desire

    Movement, sweat—quaking Kiss
        Thunder music—crushing Bliss

        Burning wicks—
          Earth's Romance
        Horizontal—
          bodies Dance

            Volcanic heat—peak, Blow
              Molten rock—faces
    Glow

      Quiet night—
        giants Tire....
          No more Wind,
              flames Expire....

PART TWO

ADULTHOOD

TIME TURNS
A.C.K.

Time turns me over
like a finished page
to act me out again one day
on some modern stage.

GLANCE OF WINE
A.C.K.

As I drink a glance of wine,
glassing out the window pane,
I dew upon the view
of the drawing, rippled rain.

SENTINEL
C.C.T.

When at last a long love is lost,
nerves begin to fray
and force deep desires aside—
hearts are not for play.

All alone here at home,
left wrapped within an ache,
crying softly through the night—
feelings we can't fake.

Then I find she's not at home
and worried who they are.
Pictures flashing in my mind—
laughter outside a bar.

Love and freedom run at angles,
then temporarily parallel.
On our own, the things we do—
tangents we'll never tell.

GLACIERS
A.C.K.

Inside me is a mammoth sound,
a noise I wish I could not hear.
Its pounding is only loud
when winter months draw near.

Inside, the sound runs me ragged, down
               then shows its salty, ice-block edge—

                     Like a massive tusk in tar, I've drowned

        in that bittersweet,
        that rebounding
                  Sound,

      swept off its gelid
Ledge.

ADVICE FROM DAD
C.C.T.

Said I never swept
the garage quite right....
A belt too loose,
or maybe too tight.

Money comes in,
then money goes out....
Someday I'll succeed, Dad,
I have no doubt.

Wake up early,
and late to bed....
Like him, I'll work
all my life till I'm dead.

No job, no money, Dad—
no one, nothing, none....
Supporting a daughter,
and now, another – a son.

Good times? I had some
a long time ago....
Now, I'm just like him;
suddenly, I feel sixty or so.

Twenty-something body,
young face, but the pain is old.
My heart is warm, but
still, emotions are cold.

Times of anger
...but mostly just sad.

Friends? Few, like him
...family no longer the family I had.

This life is depressing
and it's all 'cause of me.
I'll pick it all up, Dad—
just you wait and see.

I'll make lots of money—
see his face full of pride.
He'll say, "That's my son...
I'm sorry he died."

ICE SCREAM
A.C.K.

A racket of clattering ice hails
the metal bucket's shining walls,
and over the slick, gray blur it sails,
like a frozen, shattered Niagara Falls.

INNKEEPING THE ELDERLY
A.C.K.

Changing, washing,
Beep! Fold,
           dusting
Sweeping, keeping out the cold.
Basket, checking,
Dink! Ice,
           mopping,
Bucket, coffee twice.
Waking, lights up,
Click! Towels,
           trash cans,
Dumping, moving bowels.

CAN-TANKEROUS
A.C.K.

In the garage, reaching for Old Gray—
that battered, tinny watering can—
I asked, "But can you water?"
of the banged-up man.
He clanged against Rusty,
the dusty red wagon, in a barrage of screeching:
"Like any plastic pitcher can!"

WRITERMOUSE
A.C.K.

I am asleep when you see me
like a bat, closed
up, upside-down.
Hanging on by one leg—
sometimes two.
Ready to fall into my nightly flight.

PATH
A.C.K.

I see you,
loose stepping stone among the rows of those still whole.
What foot befell you differently alone
to break apart your soul?

LAUNDRY
A.C.K.

Fear is someone's damn laundry
waiting in that small, random
Room-Without-a-Door—
damp layers overflowing
dirtied worries onto
tiled floor.

To Hell with the well-worn fear!
Leave it hampered, like a lost
Sock-Without-its-Mate—
inside-out in a corner
while the naked escape
zippered fate.

ADULT BIRTHDAYS
A.C.K.

You receive mostly cards,
empty folds of paper shards.
Very few cards mailed
arrive on time,
and none of the damn card poems
rhyme.
There is no week-long anticipation.
The one early card is from some obscure relation
(handwriting too deplorable,
cursive words illegible,
incorrigible!)
You instead assess the card's other talents:
Patterned colors, jokes, decoraments.

You eat cake for breakfast
...and then again for lunch.
(A cake you've stolen
from some other department's work party brunch).
You eat it on a paper towel patterned with birds or just plain or maybe fish
so that you do not have to wash the dish.
Candles?
Schmandles. No longer a thing.
In the car: "Happy Birthday! Happy Birthday!"
– on the way to work and on the way home from work –
to you, yourself, you sing.

You put something extra in your coffee
(to take a special birthday shit).
You wear the favorite socks;
You check the mailbox twice for gifts.

You see how many people remember your birthday
on all the little *screens*;
Yet, so many people remember,
that Nobody Really Cares, it seems.

In fact, you care – you fear –
a little less with every year.

Your birthday is just like any other day
because every day is the same.
Then again, that could mean
that *any day* is your day of name.

Now, you realize, the older you grow,
you have 364 secret birthdays
….starting – Hell, why not? – *tomorrow.*

PEOPLE OF THE SOUTH WIND
A.C.K.

Here, in Midwest somewhere—
like a tiny speck in a dusty sunbeam—
I can feel the warm and windy
wheat-woven grasses
sway under stumpy trees and stars.

I breathe in the heavy hum of cicadas in the humid air
as I listen for the train whistle,
following gravel roads
between squares of rows and rows of nowhere.

I wade the shallow creek beds with snakes and turtles
on afternoons of wide horizons
loosely fenced
in wood and wire and a watchdog's playful bark.

Tonight, as the coyotes rally—
like a swelling blend of eerie war cries—
I witness a sudden sunset
and turn to face
the storm siren's steady wail.

LOVE FROM MOTHER
A.C.K.

It is pretty quiet
around here
without you
dropping by
and it takes me forever to finish a carton of milk.

I bought my new bird feeder
with a red roof.
Love you.

The dogs are jumping around
ready to go
outside
while I try to fix the TV.
Yesterday
your dad used the remote.

I am trying to find
a windbreaker jacket.
More later.

DEGREES
A.C.K.

We all wish our lives to be at the perfect right angle
when they are mostly acute or growing rather obtuse.
We are fearful we all end at that fateful flat line!
But there is a circular pathway drawn just for our use.

PART THREE

CIRCLES

CONFUSION
A.C.K.

At times, life is first lost
in the creases of a restless mind.
Folds and folds of gray
matter less and less, I find.

SHOWER THOUGHTS
A.C.K.

Every time I shower,
hair falls from my head.
Some days I wish it were bad thoughts
that I shed instead.
If every time I showered
bad thoughts fell from my head,
I'd be washed clean for all my days
of every single dread.

STIMULI
A.C.K.

This elbow is my hardest bend.
This heart my highest jump.
My foot, a mutual friend of plane.
My gut, a nervous dump.

Every word and phrase hung up all year
to a mind of festive lights,
and emotions rhyme the cursive letters
of memories and sights.

GRAVITY
C.C.T.

Blasting through a movement—
Grimace – while in motion:
Cable-tight coiled snake,
                power of an ocean.

Arms bronze, cut from oak—
Mountainous – peaks of glistening skin;
Mother nature starts you out,
                and that's where you begin.

Grasp of eagle's talons—
Wrapped – hands around a bar:
Explosion through a movement,
                distance, not so far.

Going down then blasting up—
Back – head held to face the sky.
A non-stop forest fire
                burning in your thigh.

LITTLE ARMORED ME
A.C.K.

I'm a hard, little Pioneer:
One
who ventures
into Unknown or Unclaimed
territory to settle.
Yet true pioneers never settle
and so
I hustle along across hot grasslands
in my awkward body—
moving with amusing energy.
Imagining little
Treasures, I entertain
myself with digging
little holes
in People
and finding for them
all their long, little Stories.
I tell myself wild tales
in my own way
alone in my shell, my
World.
I keep my heart's blood warm beneath a boundary
Guarded
from the startling fights
beyond odd little me, beyond
Special You, who I fight for
when tough hide is
Broken.
Crying, I draw myself into a Circle
whenever
I sense a storm, then—
floating on my guts through floodplain—

I Pioneer on,
the little armored
one—
Just being
Me,
the Armadillo.

A YEAR IN KANSAS
A.C.K.

It is cooler
here
now in the 80s
and rained all morning.
We are
actually having cooler mornings
now (for about 3 hours)
but
certainly, no jackets!
We are
under a thunderstorm watch
tonight.
It did get humid again
after a few days of cooler weather.
I would love
a good storm as
we are
not in tornado season.
The weather is hot again. It is
now getting cold
here.
We used the woodstove
last night
for the first time.
Have not turned on the heat
yet.
It is very cold—
15 degrees or
something.
Just a sprinkle of snow
last night.
It's finally cold

now but no snow.
I've been able to ride
the bike
to work every day.
It was a bit brisk
at 9 degrees F
this morning
at 65 miles per hour
on the highway.
The wind chill
at that temperature
and speed
is -39 degrees
F.
I think
everyone gets blah in the winter
and then again
in August
because of the heat.
This is why
Girl Scout cookies are delivered
in winter.
We actually have
snow today.
This winter has been
Snowless (not
a word) so
a small amount is
festive.
The weather
here
has been unusually temperate.
It's been the
nicest February in years.
First tornado watch.
Wondering
if this will be a long tornado season—

we are
starting early.
It's been the mildest winter
I can recall
in recent years.
Tonight
the sirens went off in town
but not in Lawrence.
The storm was south
of us. Sadly,
a tornado hit a small town
west of Topeka
and destroyed buildings.
Time to check the batteries in the storm radio.
In fact,
it is too warm
for this time of year and
that is weird.
Everything is blooming
a month early. Big
storms
here
today and tomorrow.
Put grass seed down
yesterday.
Good timing.
I was home
by 7:30 to watch tornado coverage.
I was very concerned
about the Wichita area.
When the tornado was hitting Wichita,
I was almost in tears—
from the original tracking it looked like
it would be even closer
to my sister than five miles.
But
tornadoes don't follow maps

and it tracked
slightly to the east.
We are
not getting enough
rain
here
so it could be a long summer.
It is so hot and dry in our summers
but whatever.
This is like August
which
is my least favorite
month!
No rain in the forecast
so
Tonight I will water
here. Watered the maple tree
last night.
If it gets drier,
we will have a total
burn ban.
You can only shoot off fireworks
on your own property.
This is
the second driest summer since
1911. I feel
for the people of the Depression Era,
the Dust Bowl. How defeating
that must have been.
It gets drier
here each day.
Still catching up on General Hospital
but it is so hot
that what else is there to do?
In general, plants and trees are
really suffering.
I guess this is nature's way of thinning out

the foliage.
It is finally
raining
here. I would go outside
and stand in it.
Well,
maybe not—
lightning.
It's still in the 100s
here
and no rain in sight
for the next 10 days.
Whew
….hot. Kansas
is going to be a Dust Bowl
again.
It rained in western and central
Kansas
but fell apart before it got
here.
When it's hot
I sometimes stop by that coffee
shack thing
and get a cherry snow cone.
Wild fires
in Oklahoma this past week.
Rain
is needed badly in the Midwest!
It might
rain
but I have given up
real belief in predictions
so I just go ahead
and water when I think it is due.
The drought
is very evident...
as I tried to dig, I could not

without watering the dirt first.
I will never
complain about rain
or snow again—
this has given me so much appreciation
for those naturally-occurring
events.
No rain
here
yet. They said
we wouldn't get any
hurricane rain but
now the radar looks possible.
I hope for some.
I put away all my sandals
and got the "winter"
shoes down.
It is finally
raining
here.
All morning long rain…
so lovely.
The dust was getting bad
and yesterday was very windy.
I hated it
and can only imagine
what the Dust Bowl
felt like in those old, horribly-insulted
homes.

One of the Christmas cacti is blooming—
pretty.

CIRCLES
C.C.T.

Born into life's mess:
First breath with a cry....
Ten flailing fingers and toes:
to live, then to die.

Waiting for teeth, drooling,
crawling along the floor.
You turn toward a voice:
each day, knowing more.

No walking or talking—
wispy, fine hair.
Just filling your pants
...it doesn't seem fair.

Feeding at all hours
from your Mother's breast.
Grasping tightly
and passing the test.

Food smeared all over
your face, hands, leg, chair....
Lunch belches back up,
spoon thrown in the air.

With help to stand
you wiggle into a walk.
Stumble and fall
...you *think* you can talk.

Your father looks on, and
to his surprise—

You're walking, talking—
he's awed by your size.

Moving in and out of clothing,
growing day by day.
Listening, watching,
and learning at play.

Working hard at school
to read, count, and write.
Making the grade and
doing things right.

Soon, you've made friends;
now, you're on a first date.
Life fills in and speeds up—
too little, too late.

Wedding bells peel
while the Mothers cry.
You swear before a god
that you don't swear by.

In a two-bedroom house,
you share with the One,
you ready the guest room
for a daughter or son.

Caught in circles of life:
giving birth with a sigh.
A beginning again and
your parents will die.

SEASONS
A.C.K.

Baby spring is the age of
Three
With blueberries
Squeezed in her hands:
Hopping, skipping,
Making noise—
A train of bumble-bee bands.

Youthful summer feels like a
Teen
With tense heat waves
All in your face:
Dragging, working,
Running free—
Growing quickly out of grace.

Elder autumn is a grown
Adulthood
With time and place
To leave behind:
Bearing, changing,
Falling soon—
Many memories in mind.

Dead winter tells of winters
Past
With hardened tales
Of grievous gray:
Stilling, sleeping,
Lighting fires—
Facing down the shortened day.

(OCEAN)
C.C.T.

Green-veiled blue,
capped in white:
Lethargic pounding,
a constant fight.

Pushed and pulled,
inside out:
Dynamic movement,
churning about.

Life down under,
climb outside in:
Beginning mankind
without its sin.

Floor jeweled in décor,
some big with time:
Whispered thunder
(a rhythm, a rhyme).

THIRD FRUIT FROM THE WINDOW
A.C.K.

The last peach from a wooden bowl
full of browning bananas:

I devoured its planet,
sucked till its rivers swirled,
and held, dripping, that velvet world.
Then, there, that complex pit!
I loved the spinning whole of it,
from first I ripped its crust in lust
and tore through to rock-seed core.

Give me Universe,
you fruitful Bowl, give me just one more.

A WOMAN, DYING
A.C.K.

Her eyebrows
rose over hollow bone,
furrowed over rolling lids,
rippling slightly, roving, gliding—
her darkened gaze wandered, slid
back and forth, by and by,
like a cloud's heavy shadow, hid.

Her mouth
stretched over yellowed rocks,
thinly ribboned with pale red rivers,
suspended as a cavern—
open over the buff cleft of her chin's rough cliff:
Her jagged neck shivered, groaning,
a lifelong erosion in her throat, a shift.

Her body
sunk into mired folds,
limbs left limp,
forming to the forest floor—
welcoming earth's envelope, free:
Slipping soiled into the decay.
Her shuddering last breath clattered like stones thrown down a hollow tree.

And the tip of her tongue tucked itself into the curve of the cave, an exhausted body leaning in the shelter's doorway, sweating.

DENOUMENT
A.C.K.

I find myself desperate at the denoument,
approaching the story's final stages.
I'm more at home in rambling tomes
Living forever lost in lengthy pages.

STAIRS TO NOWHERE
A.C.K.

Imagine a staircase leading up to nowhere
With the end just out of sight,
And each day adds another uncertain step,
Leading one up the flight.
Everyone journeys on separate stairs,
Tripping along their tour.
Some will gaze on-and-on and upward;
Others stare back at the floor.
We all bungle those suddenly broken steps
That one is sure to find.
Thank the clever Lord of Inclination
We can let them fall behind.
But we dredge up all our measured missteps—
Afraid to, once more, begin.
What a miserable risk it is to rise and prove
What goes down, comes up again....
Despite our failings, we still have railings.
Look up ahead—a landing!
I see you go marching on quick and sure,
But I find myself...standing.
Why, she has stairs with a cast-iron banister!
But his twist steeply and sway....
I see others trudging slow, just step-by-step
When there's plenty room to play!
Who is that stomping the life out of his stairs?
And she sands hers all the time!
But finely carved, straight or curving around—
They work as long as they climb!
Wait! I can reach out to you over my rail,
Yet I must keep on my own.
If only I could spare to share my stairs,
But each stride is mine alone.

Still, all our stairs are spiraling nowhere
Built with one intention:
To progress in all this tiresome treading,
Our only way of extension.
As we ascend to that secret "nowhere" end,
A new stairway is complete,
And we go forward toward the unknown top
To find "somewhere" to rest our feet!

ABOUT THE AUTHORS

ASHLEY CLAYTON KAY

Ashley Clayton Kay is an author-publisher, weekend blogger, novelist, and late-night poetess from Douglas County, Kansas. She enjoys wine, art, crafts, and difficult conversations. This is her first publication.

CARLIN CHARLES THOMPSON

Carlin Charles Thompson is a first-time author and long-time poet from Douglas County, Kansas. He enjoys weight-lifting, reading, renovating, and riding his motorcycle. This is his first publication.

MARCKS Publishing
www.marckspublishing.com

www.ingramcontent.com/pod-product-compliance
Lightning Source LLC
Chambersburg PA
CBHW060659030426
42337CB00017B/2699